Exploration

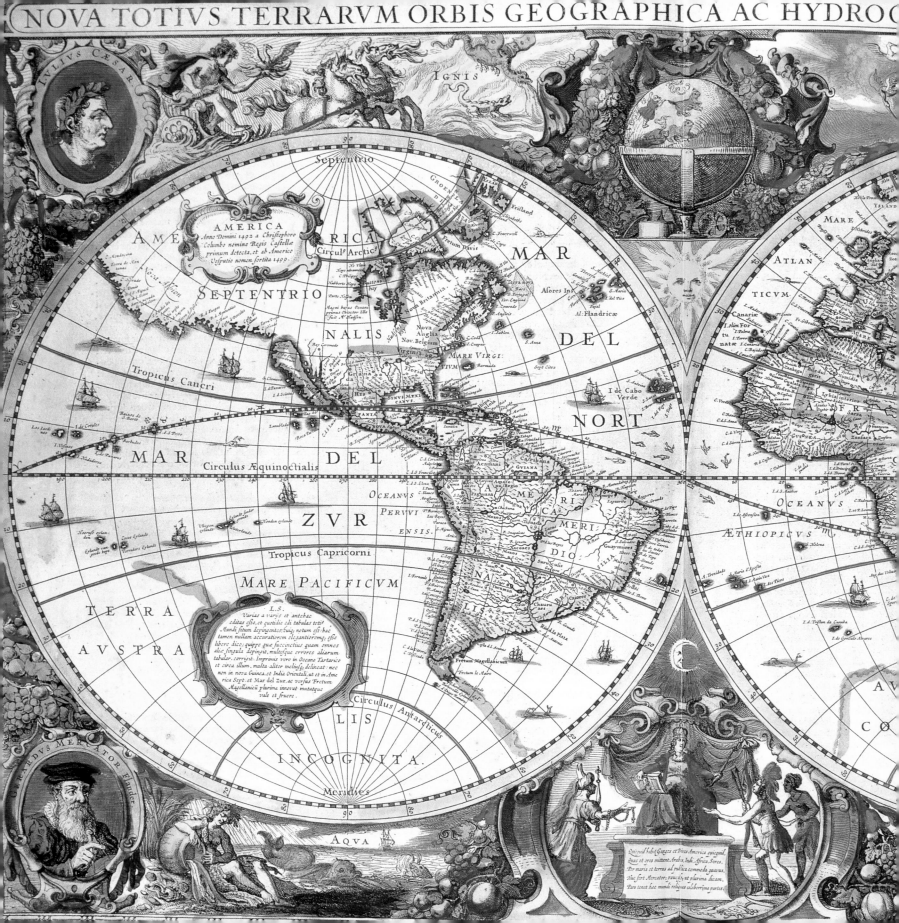

Exploration

REBECCA STEFOFF

BENCHMARK BOOKS

MARSHALL CAVENDISH
NEW YORK

✳ ✳ ✳

Benchmark Books · Marshall Cavendish Corporation · 99 White Plains Road · Tarrytown, New York 10591-9001
www.marshallcavendish.com · Copyright © 2005 Rebecca Stefoff · All rights reserved. No part of this book may be reproduced or
utilized in any form or by any means electronic or mechanical including photocopying, recording, or by any information storage and
retrieval system, without permission from the copyright holders. · All Internet sites were available and accurate when sent to press.
Library of Congress Cataloging-in-Publication Data · Stefoff, Rebecca, 1951– · Exploration / by Rebecca Stefoff. · p. cm. — (World
historical atlases) · Summary: Text plus historical and contemporary maps provide a look at the world during the Age of Exploration.
Includes bibliographical references and index. · ISBN 0-7614-1640-4 · 1. Discoveries in geography—Juvenile literature. 2.
Explorers—Juvenile literature. 3. Voyages and travels—Juvenile literature. [1. Discoveries in geography. 2. Explorers. 3. Voyages and
travels.] I. Title II. Series: Stefoff, Rebecca, 1951– . World historical atlases. · G175.S833 2004 · 910'.9—dc22 · 2003012032
Printed in China · 1 3 5 6 4 2 · Book designer: Sonia Chaghatzbanian

Picture research by Linda Sykes Picture Research, Inc., Hilton Head, SC

The photographs in this book are used by permission and through the courtesy of: Mary Evans Picture Library, London, UK: front
cover, 37; British Library, London, UK, Maps C.3.d.1: ii; Bettmann/Corbis: 6-7, 43; Antikensammlung, Munich, Germany/Erich
Lessing/Art Resource, NY: 9; Louvre, Paris, France ©RMN/Art Resource, NY: 10; Bibliotheque Nationale, Paris/Snark/Art Resource, NY:
11, 20; Philadelphia Museum of Art/Corbis: 12; British Library, London, UK, Cotton ms. Tiberius BV pt.1 f.40v: 14 Bibliotheque
Nationale, Paris/Bettmann/Corbis: 15; British Library, London, UK, Maps C.23.e.12: 17; Archivo Iconografico, S. A./Corbis: 23;
Stapleton Collection/Corbis: 25; Snark/Art Resource, NY: 27; Stefano Blanchetti/Corbis: 28; Hulton-Deutsch Collection/Corbis: 30;
Underwood and Underwood/Corbis: 32-33; Historical Picture Archive/Corbis: 34; Hulton-Deutsch/Corbis: 38; Bibliotheque Nationale,
Paris, France: back cover

Contents

CHAPTER ONE
A Widening World

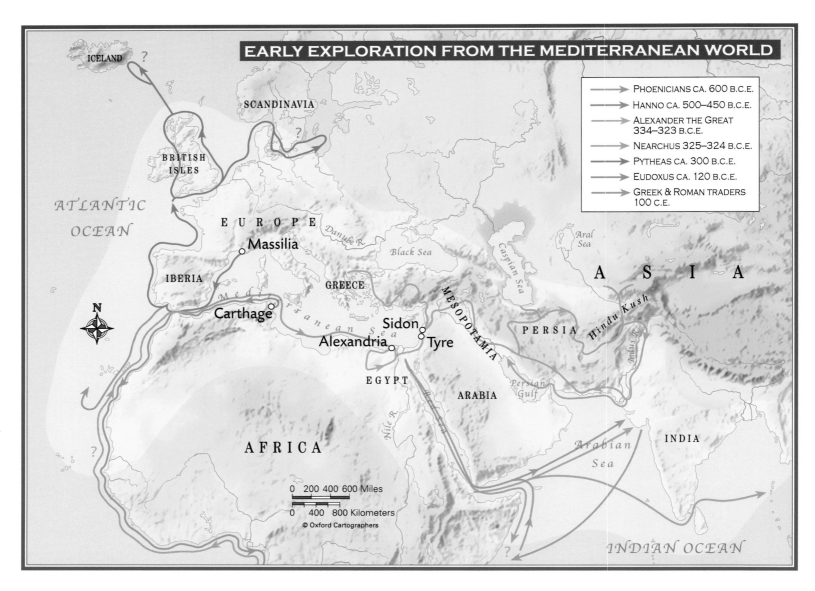

EARLY EXPLORATION FROM THE MEDITERRANEAN WORLD

ICELAND ?

SCANDINAVIA

BRITISH ISLES

ATLANTIC OCEAN

EUROPE

Danube R.

Black Sea

Massilia

Aral Sea

IBERIA

GREECE

Caspian Sea

A S I A

N

Mediterranean Sea

Carthage

Sidon

MESOPOTAMIA

PERSIA

Hindu Kush

Indus R.

Alexandria

Tyre

EGYPT

ARABIA

Persian Gulf

Nile R.

Arabian Sea

INDIA

AFRICA

?

0 200 400 600 Miles

0 400 800 Kilometers

© Oxford Cartographers

?

INDIAN OCEAN

Legend:
- PHOENICIANS CA. 600 B.C.E.
- HANNO CA. 500–450 B.C.E.
- ALEXANDER THE GREAT 334–323 B.C.E.
- NEARCHUS 325–324 B.C.E.
- PYTHEAS CA. 300 B.C.E.
- EUDOXUS CA. 120 B.C.E.
- GREEK & ROMAN TRADERS 100 C.E.

The ancient civilizations of the Mediterranean Sea knew the geography of most of Europe, North Africa, and western Asia (the highlighted area). Knowledge of these regions grew as people made journeys of exploration, trade, and conquest. A Greek named Eudoxus, for example, sailed across the Arabian Sea from Egypt to India and back. Later he set out to explore the western coast of Africa. He never returned from that voyage, and his fate is unknown.

People explored the world in three stages. First, civilizations in various regions learned about the lands beyond their borders. Later, a picture of the entire globe emerged as European seafarers crossed the oceans and charted the continental coastlines. In the final stage, explorers filled in the blank spaces on the map by entering the continental interiors and the polar regions. Mystery surrounds the earliest explorations. Information about them is scarce, often mixed with legend and rumor. Still, we know of many early travelers who advanced our geographic knowledge by going beyond their known and familiar worlds.

ANCIENT EXPLORERS

Herodotus, an ancient Greek historian writing in the fifth century B.C.E., mentioned what may have been one of the world's first major voyages of exploration. He claimed that more than a century earlier a group of Phoenicians, members of a **maritime** Mediterranean civilization, had sailed around Africa. Scholars disagree about whether such a voyage ever took place. Around 500 B.C.E., though, another Phoenician expedition sailed to west Africa. Under their leader, Hanno, the Phoenicians established trading colonies along the African coast.

Another early voyager was a Greek named Pytheas, who wrote a book about a journey he made around 300 B.C.E. The book has been lost, but scraps of Pytheas's story can be found in the works of other

A decoration from a Greek wine cup, made around 540 B.C.E., shows the god Dionysus lounging on the deck of his ship. Actual Greek ships, while they did not take the shape of a fish, were similar in style to this fanciful vessel of the gods.

Describing the World

As the Greeks learned more about the world around them, they wrote books on geography and made increasingly detailed maps. In *Travels around the World*, written in about 500 B.C.E., a scholar named Hecateus described the earth as a huge circular landmass, with Greece and the Mediterranean Sea in the middle and a ring of ocean around the outer edge. A few hundred years later, most educated Greeks knew that the earth was a sphere. Eratosthenes, a librarian in the Greek city of Alexandria in Egypt, accurately estimated the distance around it. In about 100 B.C.E., however, Poseidonius of Rhodes argued that the earth was shaped like an egg, not a sphere, and smaller than Eratosthenes had claimed. The most influential ancient geographer, Ptolemy of Alexandria, returned to the notion that the world was round but agreed with Poseidonius about its size. Written about 150 C.E., Ptolemy's *Geography* shaped people's views of the world for many centuries. It led some European explorers, including Christopher Columbus, to believe that the world was smaller than it is.

Claudius Ptolemaus, known as Ptolemy, was the ancient world's most important geographer. A Greek who lived and worked in Alexandria, Egypt, he wrote the first known scientific work on map-making. None of Ptolemy's own maps survive, but in the thirteenth century C.E. Europeans began basing their maps on his ideas about world geography.

writers. Pytheas sailed along Europe's Atlantic coast and reached Britain, where he heard about a northern land called Thule. He claimed to have visited Thule, which may have been Iceland or Scandinavia.

Meanwhile the Greeks were learning more about Asia. Between 334 and 323 B.C.E. the ruler Alexander the Great led an army through the Persian **empire** of western Asia and beyond. He and his men marched through Afghanistan to the Indus River in what is now Pakistan. On the return trip Nearchus, one of Alexander's generals, commanded a fleet that sailed the Arabian Sea and the Persian Gulf. Within a few centuries Greek and Roman explorers and traders would sail to ports in India and east Africa.

CHINESE TRAVELERS

Over a 1,500-year period, travelers from the Chinese empire made far-ranging journeys across Asia on religious pilgrimages and political missions. Some who returned to China wrote about their explorations, giving readers glimpses of the rest of the world.

Between 138 and 114 B.C.E. the emperor of China sent a diplomat named Zhang Qian (or Chang Ch'ien) on two trips beyond China's western frontier to forge alliances between China and tribes in central Asia and Iran. Zhang failed in this mission, but he spent years studying the geography, people, and economy of central Asia. His reports to the emperor led to the opening of the Silk Road, a **caravan** trade route that linked northern China with western Asia and the eastern Mediterranean for more than a thousand years.

China's long seacoast and large rivers encouraged the development of shipbuilding and navigation. The Chinese became expert sailors. They were also skilled mapmakers, although their maps seldom showed much of the world beyond China's borders.

A Chinese admiral named Zheng He commanded several voyages to the Indian Ocean. He returned to China with gifts for the emperor from India and Africa. Exotic new animals such as giraffes created great excitement in the Chinese court.

Xuan Zang (Hsuan-tsang) spent the years from 629 to 645 C.E. traveling from China to India and back to study the Indian religion Buddhism. He covered thousands of miles by land and sea; collected thousands of sacred books and paintings; and survived desert heat, pirate attacks, and hazardous mountain crossings. Back in China, Xuan wrote a book that gave the Chinese their first detailed look at India.

Between 1405 and 1433 an admiral named Zheng He (Cheng Ho) commanded a series of naval missions. He had two goals: to explore the lands around the South China Sea and the Indian Ocean and to impress the people of those lands with China's glory, wealth, and power. The largest expedition may have had more than 100 ships and 30,000 men. Several ships from this fleet reached ports in the Red Sea and on Africa's east coast. This was the first known direct contact between the Chinese and African peoples.

VIKING VOYAGES

Between 800 and 1100 C.E., Europe's best shipbuilders and sailors were the Vikings, seafarers from Norway, Denmark, and Sweden. The most daring seafarers were

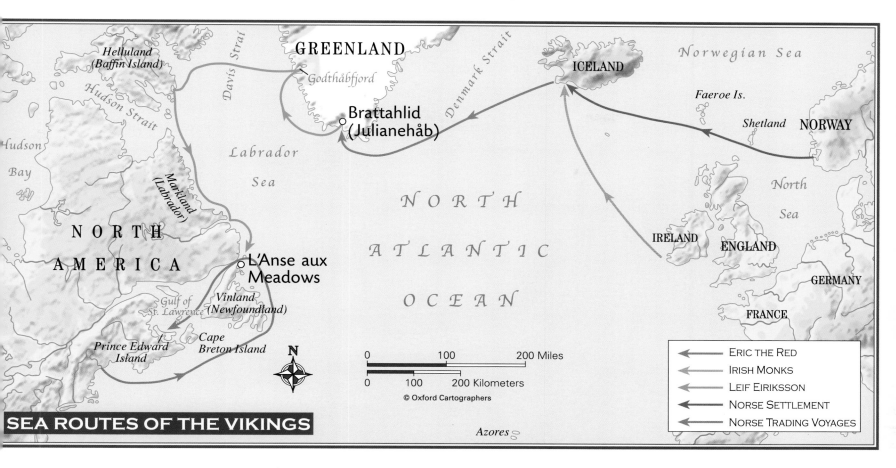

SEA ROUTES OF THE VIKINGS

Map labels: Helluland (Baffin Island), Davis Strait, GREENLAND, Godthåbfjord, Denmark Strait, ICELAND, Norwegian Sea, Faeroe Is., Shetland, NORWAY, Hudson Strait, Brattahlid (Julianehåb), Labrador Sea, North Sea, Hudson Bay, Markland (Labrador), NORTH AMERICA, L'Anse aux Meadows, IRELAND, ENGLAND, GERMANY, NORTH ATLANTIC OCEAN, Gulf of St. Lawrence, Vinland (Newfoundland), FRANCE, Prince Edward Island, Cape Breton Island, N, Azores

Scale: 0 — 100 — 200 Miles / 0 — 100 — 200 Kilometers
© Oxford Cartographers

Legend:
- ERIC THE RED
- IRISH MONKS
- LEIF EIRIKSSON
- NORSE SETTLEMENT
- NORSE TRADING VOYAGES

Norse Vikings made daring journeys across the North Atlantic Ocean. They often established colonies on the islands they discovered along the way. Although Irish monks are also believed to have made early voyages to Iceland, the Vikings founded the first permanent settlements there. Iceland was the starting point for the colonization of Greenland. But Greenland's harsh climate and slim resources doomed the colonies, which did not survive beyond the fifteenth century.

the Norsemen, Vikings from Norway. Short of space in their homeland, some Norsemen crossed storm-tossed seas to settle the Orkney, Shetland, and Faeroe islands in the North Atlantic. Then they ventured farther west and settled a larger island, Iceland. In 986 a Viking leader named Erik the Red established a colony on the huge island he named Greenland.

No sooner had the Norse settled in Greenland than a new frontier opened. A trader was bound from Iceland for the Greenland **colony** when a storm blew his ship off course. He sighted an unknown shore to the west, but instead of heading for it he returned to his original course and soon reached the Greenland colony. His story interested the Viking settlers there because the coast he had seen was forested. Greenland is treeless, so wood was rare and

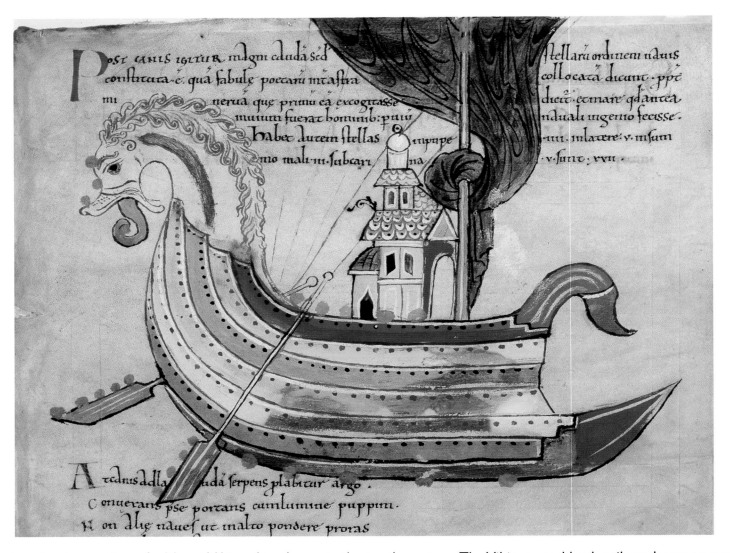

An imaginative version of a Norse Viking ship, drawn in the tenth century. The Vikings used both sails and oars to power their vessels. Viking ships handled well in both open ocean and shallow water. After making a sea crossing, the Vikings could use the same vessels to sail far up rivers to attack cities such as Paris.

precious to the colonists. Leif Erikson, son of Erik the Red, decided to investigate this tempting western shore. He set sail around 1000.

Norse writings called sagas, written down hundreds of years later, say that Erikson landed in three places that he called Helluland (Land of Flat Stones), Markland (Land of Forests), and Vinland (Land of Grapes or Wine). Most scholars believe that what Erikson discovered were the coasts of Baffin Island, Labrador, and Newfoundland. **Archaeologists** support the claim that "Vinland" was Newfoundland. Ruins of a Norse camp or settlement at L'Anse aux Meadows on the northern tip of the island date from 1010 to 1025. Greenlanders seem to have used the spot as an occasional base for hunting, exploring, or cutting timber. Although the Vikings did not create a lasting settlement in North America, they were the first Europeans to reach the continent.

THE JOURNEY OF MARCO POLO

Marco Polo of Venice, Italy, was the most famous European traveler of the late Middle Ages. He was a teenager in 1271 when he set out with his merchant father and uncle to cross Asia. The Polos reached China, where Marco spent years working for Kublai Khan, ruler of the Mongol empire that covered much of Asia. The Polos returned to Venice in 1295, traveling most of the way by sea.

A writer named Rustichello published Polo's story as a book, which immediately became wildly popular. Readers thrilled to Polo's descriptions of Kublai's splendid court, the canals and cities of China, and the exotic customs of people from Afghanistan to Vietnam. The real importance of Polo's story, however, lay in its lavish descriptions of Asian riches: the spices of India, the silks of China, the gold of Japan (a land Polo had heard about but never visited). Europeans became more eager than ever to trade with the Indies, as they called eastern and southern Asia. They also grew more impatient with the long and risky overland route. Some modern historians think that Polo may have exaggerated or even made up his story. Whether

The Catalan atlas is a set of twelve hand-painted maps completed in 1375 by Abraham Cresques, a Jewish mapmaker who lived on the Mediterranean island of Palma, near Spain. The maps were made for the king of France, and Cresques decorated them with magnificent drawings. This portion of the atlas shows Niccolo and Maffeo Polo, Marco Polo's father and uncle, traveling across Asia with their caravan and a host of Mongol escorts.

Monks, Mongols, and a Mystery

Marco Polo was not the first European of his time to cross Asia and visit the Mongol empire. Several European monks traveled from France to Mongolia, carrying messages of peace from the pope. In his book about his journey, one of those monks mentioned a mystery that had teased Europeans for more than a century. Rumors told of a powerful Christian king named Prester John who ruled an unknown land east of Persia (modern Iran). European rulers had even received a letter supposedly written by Prester John, in which the mysterious king had boasted of his wealth and might. Europeans were fighting the Muslims of the Middle East and wanted Prester John's help. The monks who went east were assigned to look for him. One of them wrote that the tales about Prester John were exaggerated, but he added that perhaps they were about a minor Mongol prince who had some Christian subjects. Marco Polo wrote that Prester John had existed but was dead. Despite these disappointments, Europeans did not abandon the myth of Prester John's kingdom. Once they realized that it did not exist in central Asia or China, they simply shifted it to a place they had not yet explored. For centuries, mapmakers placed Prester John's nonexistent kingdom in Africa.

Europeans were slow to give up the belief that a powerful Christian emperor ruled from his domain somewhere in Asia or Africa. The Latin title of this map of Africa, created by Dutch mapmaker Abraham Ortelius in 1573, translates to "Abyssinia, the Empire of Prester John."

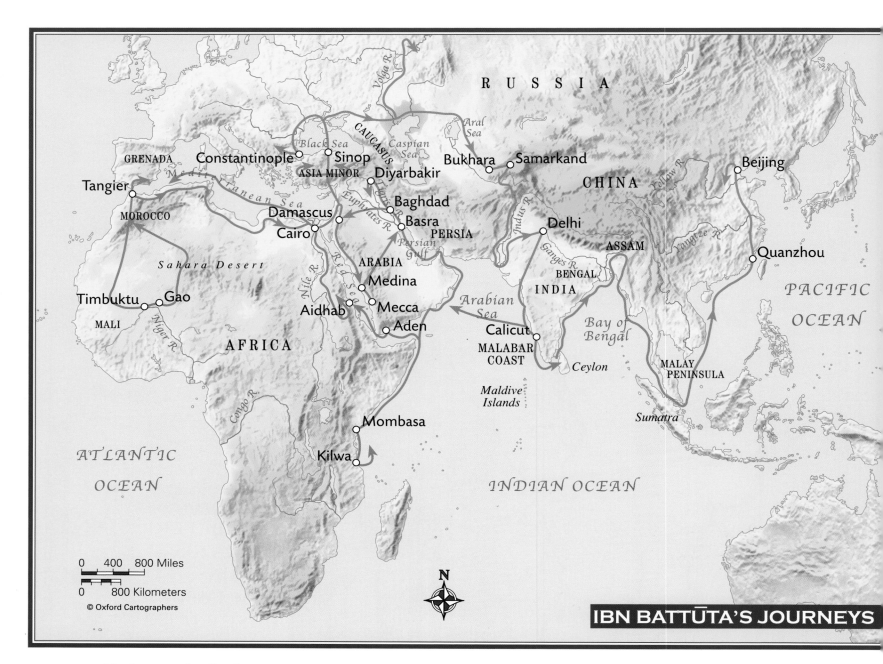

IBN BATTŪTA'S JOURNEYS

0 400 800 Miles

0 800 Kilometers

© Oxford Cartographers

Muslim traveler Ibn Battūta tried never to use the same road twice. Guided by this rule, he covered an immense amount of territory during his decades of travel. His most difficult journey was crossing the Sahara Desert to reach the African kingdom of Mali. "I have never known a more unpleasant route than this," he wrote.

or not it was true, though, it was certainly influential. Fascinating accounts such as Polo's inspired Europeans to seek out sea routes to Asia.

IBN BATTŪTA EXPLORES THE ISLAMIC WORLD

The farthest-ranging traveler of the Middle Ages was Ibn Battūta, a Muslim from Tangier in the North African country of Morocco. In 1325, at the age of twenty-one, Ibn Battūta left home to make a **pilgrimage** to the holy cities in Arabia and to study with Islamic scholars in the Near East. He enjoyed the trip so much that he yearned "to travel through the earth," as he later wrote. With his family's wealth and the income he earned as a traveling judge, Ibn Battūta spent most of the next thirty years traveling. He visited most of the world's Islamic territories and was almost always received as an honored guest. In countries that were not Islamic, he often found hospitality in Muslim communities.

Ibn Battūta blazed no new trails and made no important geographic discoveries. Unlike some explorers, he traveled in comfort, accompanied by his wives, children, and servants, moving from place to place in caravans or merchant ships. Still,

Ibn Battūta was an explorer in spirit, full of curiosity about the beliefs, pastimes, and societies of people everywhere. In journeys that carried him from Spain to Timbuktu and from Russia's Volga River to Southeast Asia and China, Ibn Battūta traveled an estimated 75,000 miles (120,750 kilometers). After settling down for good in Morocco in 1353, he dictated a book about his travels. Called the *Rihlah* (Book of Journeys), it is a rich source of information about culture, religion, and government in North Africa and Asia during the late Middle Ages.

The Great Age of European Exploration

In the fifteenth and sixteenth centuries, Europeans launched a series of sea voyages that dramatically enlarged their knowledge of the world. Several forces set those voyages in motion. Improvements in shipbuilding and **navigation** made ocean travel easier and safer. The growing power and wealth of western European states made them ambitious to claim new territories and expand the reach of Christianity. Above all, the desire for new markets and trade routes led Europeans to Africa, the Americas, and the Pacific Ocean. One result of this burst of exploration was a new understanding of world geography, as the outlines and sizes of the continents slowly came into focus. Another result was that Europeans claimed huge overseas territories, shaping the future histories of nations from Mexico to Malaysia.

THE PORTUGUESE NAVIGATORS

By around 1270 or so, Mediterranean fishermen, explorers, and traders were sailing out into the Atlantic Ocean. Some headed for the ports of England and northern Europe. Others went south and west, pioneering routes to the eastern Atlantic island clusters known as Madeira, the Canary Islands, and the Azores. Each of these island chains was well known by 1380.

In 1434 a Portuguese mariner named Gil Eanes sailed along the northwestern African coast to a point near the Canaries. Soon other Portuguese expeditions were inching ever farther along that coast, which was completely unknown to Europeans. These traders hoped to avoid using the slow caravans that carried African gold overland across the Sahara Desert to Mediterranean ports. They wanted to get the gold directly from its sources south of the desert. By the 1460s the Portuguese had succeeded in opening trading posts along the west African coast, obtaining not only gold but ivory, slaves, and pepper. In 1482 a navigator named Diogo Cão entered the mouth of the Congo River. On another voyage three years later, he almost reached the tip of southern Africa.

The Portuguese had several reasons for continuing to explore southward along Africa's west coast. They hoped to find the kingdom of the mythical Prester John. Even more important, they began to question Ptolemy's ideas about world geography. Ptolemy had said that southern Africa and Asia were joined by land, which would make it impossible to sail from the Atlantic

In the thirteenth century, Portuguese shipbuilders began building new kinds of vessels well suited to long ocean voyages. These small, compact ships—often called caravels, although there were many styles and names—typically handled rough seas better than the large cargo vessels used in Mediterranean trade. In addition to the traditional square sails, the new ships had triangular, slanted sails. Called lateen sails, they made it easier to steer the vessels in changing winds. These advances in design aided nations such as Portugal in their desire to add to their overseas holdings. Here caravels battle along the coast of what would become Portugal's most profitable colony—Brazil.

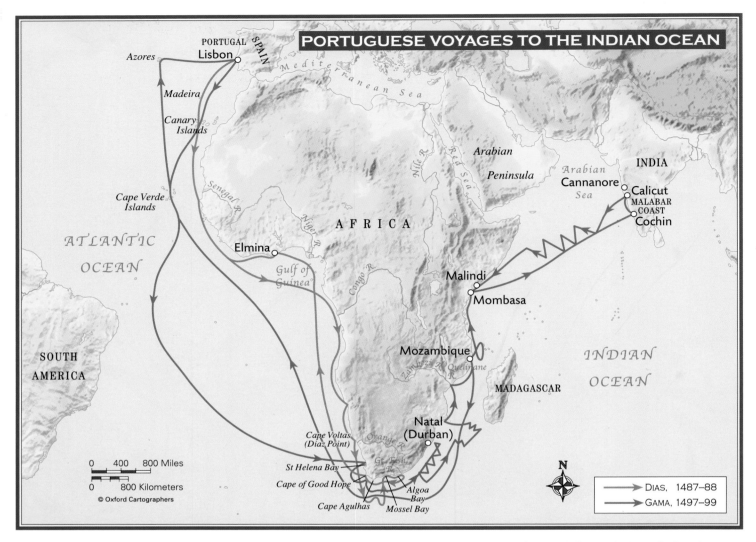

PORTUGUESE VOYAGES TO THE INDIAN OCEAN

Bartolomeu Dias led the way around the Cape of Good Hope, and Vasco da Gama followed close behind, commanding the first maritime expedition to India. Gama planned to follow Dias's route to the cape, but Dias correctly suggested that he might catch more favorable winds if he headed west, farther into the Atlantic Ocean, away from the African coast. Another Portuguese captain, Pedro Alvars Cabral, set sail for India in 1500. He also followed Dias's advice, but he led his ships so far west that he bumped into the South American coast. His unexpected landing there helped pave the way for the Portuguese colonization of Brazil.

Ocean to the Indian Ocean around the southern tip of Africa. But if Ptolemy were wrong, Europeans *might* be able to sail around Africa to the ports and spice markets of the Indies beyond. In the summer of 1487, King João II of Portugal sent

Bartolomeu Dias south with three ships and orders to find an ocean route around Africa.

TO THE INDIES

After Dias passed the farthest point that Cão had reached, a storm raged for days,

Vasco da Gama was the first explorer to sail from western Europe to India. But his goal was trade, not increasing geographic knowledge. The helmet in this portrait is a reminder that he and other European explorers of his time often accomplished their goals through military might.

Portugal in 1488, he sighted the Cape of Good Hope, the mountainous stretch that marks the southernmost point in Africa.

In 1497 Vasco da Gama led a fleet of four Portuguese ships and 170 men on the first trading voyage to Asia along the route that Dias had discovered. Gama's fleet survived the voyage to the Cape of Good Hope, although the ships were out of sight of land for more than three months—a disturbing experience for sailors used to sticking close to coastlines. Gama landed at ports in east Africa—getting into fights with several local rulers—and then sailed to India with the help of an Arab pilot who knew the sea route. Gama's cheap trade goods failed to impress the rulers and merchants of the Indian states, and he was forced to return to Portugal with a fraction of the spices he had hoped to carry. Still, Gama's voyage made him famous in Europe, and it set Portugal on a course of conquest and colonization in east Africa and the Indies.

THE UNEXPECTED AMERICAS

Between Dias's and Gama's voyages, an Italian navigator in the service of Spain also sailed for the Indies, but not by the

blowing him south into unknown waters. Dias had to sail north to find the African coast again. After cruising along the coast for several days, he realized that the shoreline west of him was running northward, which meant that he had sailed around the continent's southern tip. On his return to

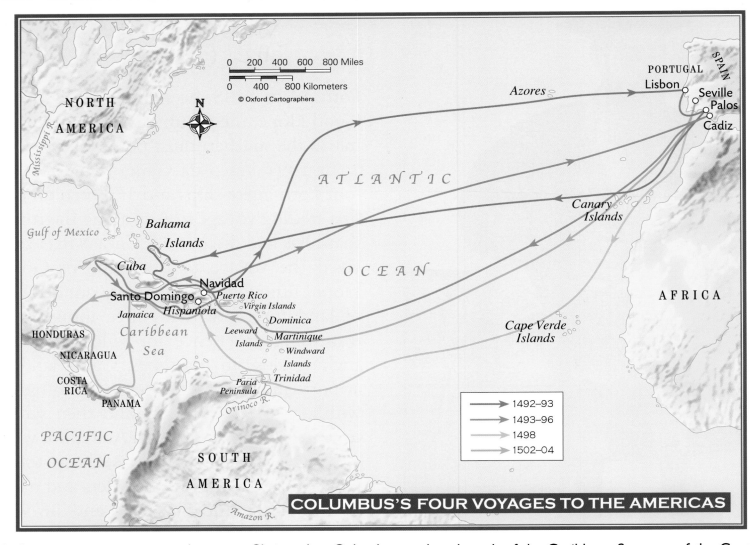

COLUMBUS'S FOUR VOYAGES TO THE AMERICAS

Map labels: NORTH AMERICA, Mississippi R., Gulf of Mexico, Bahama Islands, Cuba, Navidad, Santo Domingo, Hispaniola, Jamaica, Puerto Rico, Virgin Islands, Dominica, Leeward Islands, Martinique, Windward Islands, Trinidad, Caribbean Sea, HONDURAS, NICARAGUA, COSTA RICA, PANAMA, PACIFIC OCEAN, Paria Peninsula, Orinoco R., SOUTH AMERICA, Amazon R., ATLANTIC OCEAN, Azores, Canary Islands, Cape Verde Islands, AFRICA, PORTUGAL, Lisbon, SPAIN, Seville, Palos, Cadiz

Scale: 0 200 400 600 800 Miles / 0 400 800 Kilometers / © Oxford Cartographers

Legend: 1492–93, 1493–96, 1498, 1502–04

In four voyages spanning twelve years, Christopher Columbus explored much of the Caribbean Sea, part of the Central American coast, and a bit of the South American coast. He also founded the settlements of Navidad and Santo Domingo on the island of Hispaniola and served—rather unsuccessfully—as administrator of the island colony. This series of achievements failed to satisfy Columbus, who was determined to find the rich ports of Asia. Until his death he claimed that the lands he had explored were actually the eastern edge of the Indies.

African route. Christopher Columbus believed that by sailing west from Europe he could reach Japan and the other eastern Asian lands mentioned by Marco Polo. He would have succeeded, except for two things. First, he underestimated the size of the earth and the distance between western Europe and eastern Asia. Second, although he expected to discover new islands or countries along the way, he did not foresee that his path would be blocked by two large and completely unknown continents.

Those continents, of course, were North and South America. Yet Columbus, who had promised the Spanish king and queen a route to the Indies, argued that

A portrait of Vasco Núñez de Balboa surrounded by images of the native residents of Panama. Balboa was the first European to cross the Americas and reach the ocean that he called the South Sea and which we now refer to as the Pacific. Balboa sparked a new phase of European exploration when he first sighted the vast western waters. The conquest of the Pacific, however, would demand many voyages, many lives, and several centuries.

The Unluckiest Explorer?

Many explorers have met grim fates, but Vasco Núñez de Balboa was one of the unluckiest. Balboa was a conquistador, one of the Spanish military explorers who conquered territory in the Caribbean, Mexico, and Central and South America in the decades after Columbus's voyages. Hoping to make his fortune in Spain's American colonies, Balboa experienced a series of disasters, including bankruptcy and shipwreck. He managed to become the leader of a new settlement called Darién in Panama, but in doing so he made powerful enemies. One of them arranged to have Balboa convicted of treason and publicly beheaded in 1519. Balboa's fame as an explorer rests on a journey he had made six years earlier. Learning from the Indians that a great body of water lay west of Panama's mountainous spine, Balboa set out with a force of Spanish soldiers and Indians to investigate. After days of climbing steep mountains and crossing thick rain forests, Balboa came to a high ridge, gazed westward, and saw a limitless sea. He was the first European to look from the Americas onto the Pacific Ocean, which he called the South Sea. Even as an explorer, however, Balboa had bad luck. Three centuries after his death, the English poet John Keats wrote a sonnet about that first glimpse of the Pacific. "On First Looking into Chapman's Homer" became famous—but Keats mistakenly gave the credit for Balboa's feat to another conquistador, Hernán Cortés, the conqueror of Mexico.

they were part of Asia. He made three more voyages, searching with growing desperation for the Asian cities and people that Polo and other overland travelers had described. To the bitter end Columbus tried to convince everyone that the western lands were simply unfamiliar Asian realms. He looked in vain for a **strait** that would take him past these inconvenient obstacles. Even before Columbus died, however, other explorers had realized that the western lands Columbus had found were new to geography—the "New World" that would continue to lure Europeans for centuries.

AROUND THE WORLD

Once Europeans knew that an ocean lay west of the Americas, they expected to find the Indies on its far side. All they had to do was find a way through or around the American continents.

Many explorers searched in vain for a strait leading westward, probing every bay and river mouth on the Atlantic coasts of the Americas. Success finally came to Ferdinand Magellan. He was a Portuguese navigator who led a Spanish expedition of five ships and about 250 men south along the coast of South America in search of the eagerly sought passage from the Atlantic to

Ferdinand Magellan led his fleet on the first voyage around the world. Magellan would not enjoy the rewards of his success, though, as he died midvoyage somewhere in the Philippines.

that western sea. In 1520, after spending seven weeks exploring a turbulent route that threaded through a maze of islands at the southern tip of the continent, he emerged into the calm waters of the South Sea, which he gratefully and optimistically renamed the Pacific, meaning "peaceful." The passage he had found is now called the Strait of Magellan.

Magellan's fleet crossed the Pacific, appalled by its immense size, and eventually reached Asia. Although Magellan died in the Philippines and most of his men perished during the voyage as well, one ship and some of his crew returned to Spain by way of the Indian and Atlantic oceans. They were the first people known to have sailed around the world. The next **circumnavigation,** from 1577 to 1580, was accomplished by the Englishman Francis Drake. Magellan, Drake, and many other European explorers proved that Columbus had been right: it was possible to reach Asia by sailing west from Europe. But it wasn't easy. For centuries, crossing the Pacific—a vast stretch of ocean with very few islands to provide food and water—was a daring and hazardous trip.

I N T O   T H E   P A C I F I C

After Magellan's voyage Spain claimed the Philippines. Soon ships regularly sailed between Spain's American and Philippine colonies. Their captains gathered information about the wind and water currents of the Pacific and learned of the quickest routes. Portuguese and English navigators also traveled into the Pacific, mapping the islands they found.

In the early eighteenth century, though, European maps of the Pacific remained incomplete and inaccurate. The coasts of northeastern Asia and northwestern North America were blank or filled with guesswork. Some geographers, for example, believed that the two continents were joined at the northern edge of the Pacific. To the south, sailors had seen isolated bits of the Australian coast but did not know how these stretches of coastline were related to one another. Were they many small islands or parts of a single continent? Most mapmakers filled the southern Pacific with an enormous landmass they called the *Terra Incognita Australis,* or Unknown Southern Land. They placed it there because Ptolemy had said that it existed and because they thought the world needed it to "balance" the mass of the northern continents.

France and England sent expeditions to

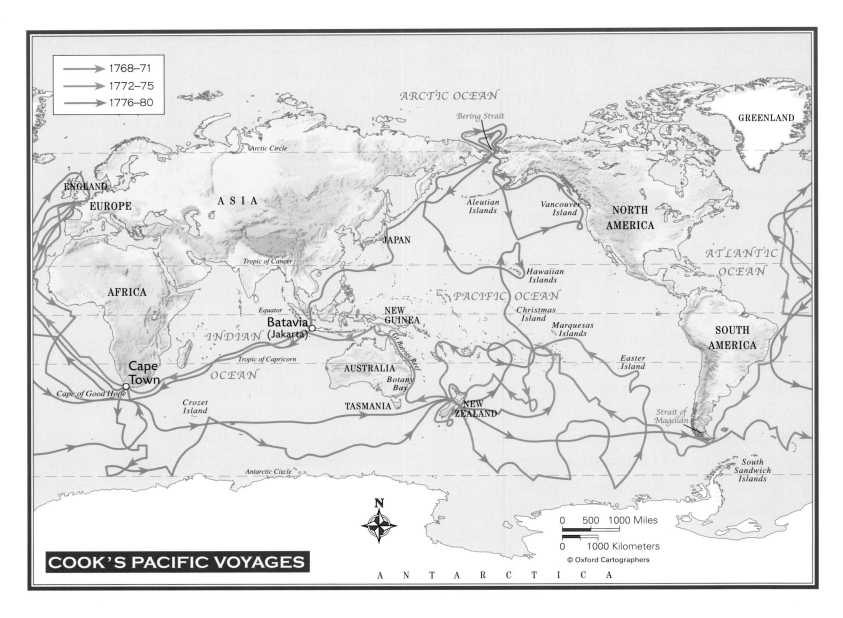

COOK'S PACIFIC VOYAGES

Legend:
- 1768–71
- 1772–75
- 1776–80

James Cook, a member of the British navy, explored and mapped much of the Pacific Ocean, from Alaska to Antarctica. His voyages proved that most of the Southern Hemisphere was open ocean and that the continents of Asia and North America do not meet at the northern edge of the Pacific, as some geographers believed.

On each of his voyages James Cook was joined by scientists, who gathered samples of plants and animals, and artists, who drew and painted pictures of the Pacific region's many creatures, people, and scenes. Here the English explorer examines the massive sculptures created by the native peoples of Easter Island.

further explore the Pacific in the eighteenth century. The most important were the three voyages led by British navigator James Cook between 1768 and 1779. Cook searched the southernmost parts of the Pacific as far as the Antarctic Circle, proving that the *Terra Incognita Australis* did not exist (although he correctly predicted the existence of the much smaller Antarctic continent). In the north he passed through the Bering Strait to the Arctic Ocean, confirming that Asia and North America were indeed separate continents. Cook mapped part of the Australian coast and much of the northwestern American coast. He was also the European discoverer of Hawaii, where he died in 1779. Cook, whose explorations answered many questions about the world's largest ocean, is now considered the most successful maritime explorer of his day.

CHAPTER THREE
Filling in the Blanks

A character in Joseph Conrad's 1902 story *Heart of Darkness* says, "Now when I was a little chap I had a passion for maps. I would look for hours at South America, or Africa, or Australia, and lose myself in the glories of exploration. At that time there were many blank spaces on the earth. . . ." The third stage of world exploration involved filling in those blanks in the hearts of continents and in the polar regions. In a sense this stage of exploration—coming to understand the world more fully and in greater detail—continues today with the study of regions such as the deep sea, the tropical forests, and space.

AMERICAN INTERIORS

Long after mariners had charted and named features along the North and South American coastlines, maps of the continents' interiors were still mostly blank, often labeled "Unknown Territory." The Spanish conquistadors filled in some of the blanks. In the early 1540s Francisco Vásquez de Coronado explored the American Southwest, and Hernando de Soto led an army on raids through the Southeast. Both sought treasure; neither found it. But along the way they gained

geographic knowledge that made its way onto European maps of North America. Around the same time an expedition led by Francisco de Orellana made the first journey by boat down South America's Amazon River.

The exploration of South America was carried out mainly by the Spanish and Portuguese, who claimed almost all of the continent. Missionaries traveled into unknown regions to convert the Indians to Christianity, while other explorers looked for gold, diamonds, or rich native civilizations to conquer. During the eighteenth century, scientists from many European countries were drawn to South America's lush tropical forests. Scientific exploration, driven by the urge to collect rare plant and animal specimens, continued into the nineteenth century, especially along the Amazon, which remains an important center of biological research to this day.

The interior of North America was not fully mapped until the nineteenth century. In 1793 Scotsman Alexander Mackenzie completed the first European crossing of North America, traveling through Canada. After reading about Mackenzie's journey, American president Thomas Jefferson wanted Americans to accomplish the same

Travelers meet Indians in the American West. Meetings such as this ended sometimes in friendly trade, sometimes in fighting. The exploration of the American interior helped end the traditional way of life of the Native American peoples, whose lands were seized by European colonial powers and, later, by the U.S. government.

feat. Under his orders Meriwether Lewis and William Clark led an American expedition that crossed the continent from 1804 to 1806. In the 1840s an American army officer named John Charles Frémont made several long journeys through the Rocky Mountains, the western deserts, and California. The reports of these expeditions inspired thousands of Americans to settle in the West. Later in the century, John Wesley Powell led the first boat trip down the Colorado River through the Grand Canyon in 1869. He then spent years exploring the rugged area where Colorado, Utah, Arizona, and New Mexico meet.

AFRICAN RIDDLES

Europeans had known a little about Egypt and North Africa since ancient times, but the region south of the Sahara Desert remained a mystery to them. In the late

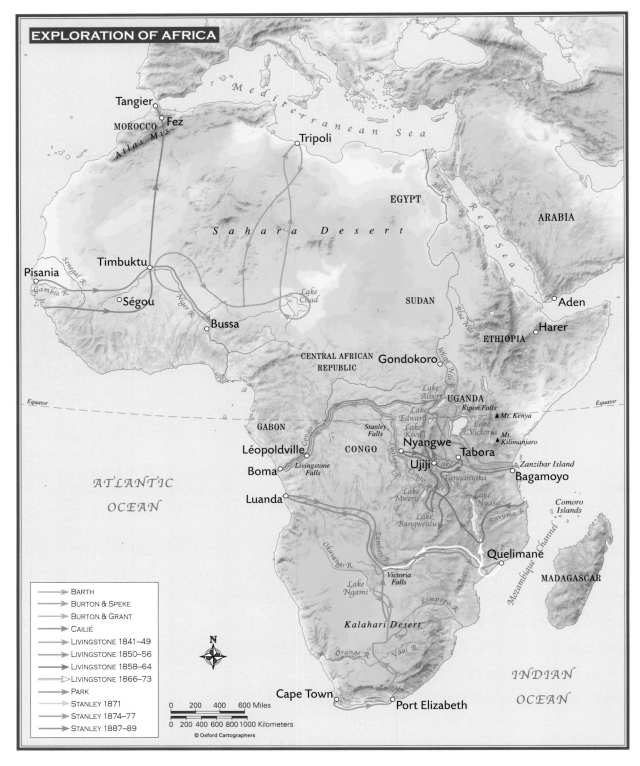

EXPLORATION OF AFRICA

Tangier
Fez
MOROCCO
Atlas Mts.
Tripoli

Mediterranean Sea

EGYPT

Nile R.

Red Sea

ARABIA

Sahara Desert

Pisania
Senegal R.
Gambia R.
Timbuktu
Ségou
Niger R.
Bussa

Lake Chad

SUDAN

Aden

Blue Nile R.

Harer

ETHIOPIA

Equator

CENTRAL AFRICAN REPUBLIC

Gondokoro
White Nile R.

GABON

Congo R.

Léopoldville
Boma
Livingstone Falls

Luanda

Lake Albert
Lake Edward
Lake Kivi
Stanley Falls
UGANDA
Ripon Falls
Mt. Kenya
Lake Victoria
Mt. Kilimanjaro

Nyangwe
Lualaba R.
Ujiji
Congo R.
Tabora
Lake Tanganyika
Zanzibar Island
Bagamoyo

Lake Mweru

Lake Bangweulu

Lake Nyasa

Ruvuma R.

Comoro Islands

Okavango R.
Zambezi R.
Victoria Falls
Quelimane
Mozambique Channel
MADAGASCAR

ATLANTIC OCEAN

Lake Ngami

Kalahari Desert

Orange R.
Vaal R.
Limpopo R.

INDIAN OCEAN

Cape Town
Port Elizabeth

Legend

- → BARTH
- → BURTON & SPEKE
- → BURTON & GRANT
- → CAILIÉ
- → LIVINGSTONE 1841–49
- → LIVINGSTONE 1850–56
- → LIVINGSTONE 1858–64
- → LIVINGSTONE 1866–73
- → PARK
- → STANLEY 1871
- → STANLEY 1874–77
- → STANLEY 1887–89

N

0   200   400   600 Miles
0 200 400 600 800 1000 Kilometers

© Oxford Cartographers

Africa swarmed with European explorers during the nineteenth century. Heinrich Barth of Germany traveled across North Africa. In addition to mapping Nigeria and Mali and crossing the Sahara Desert several times, Barth recorded the vocabularies of many local languages. René Cailié of France reached the ancient city of Timbuktu, then off-limits to Christians, by disguising himself as a Muslim pilgrim. On expeditions with Richard Francis Burton and James Grant, British army officer John Hanning Speke traced the course of the Nile River. One result of this wave of exploration was that the European powers claimed colonies in almost every part of Africa, dividing the continent among them.

eighteenth century, Europeans began pushing farther and farther into the African interior. Scientific or geographic curiosity drove some of them. But Europeans were mostly interested in claiming colonial territory and discovering new sources of timber, minerals, and other natural resources. By the nineteenth century slavery also played a role in African exploration. Just as the slave trade had drawn Europeans to Africa in earlier centuries, the desire to end the slave trade drew missionaries and reformers into central Africa. They believed that a European presence was needed there to put a stop to capturing and selling slaves. Scottish missionary-explorer David Livingstone, for example, explored remote and unknown parts of Africa to discover how the slave trade was carried out, and by whom.

For centuries Africa had presented geographers with riddles. From contact with the Saharan caravan trade, Europeans knew that a large river called the Niger flowed through west Africa. But they did not know its route or where it reached the sea. Was it the same as the Congo River? Geographers also wondered where the source of Egypt's Nile River was found. The ancient geographer Ptolemy said that

it flowed from two huge lakes fed by streams from a range he called the Mountains of the Moon. Could this range be the source of rumors that tropical Africa had mountains with snowy peaks?

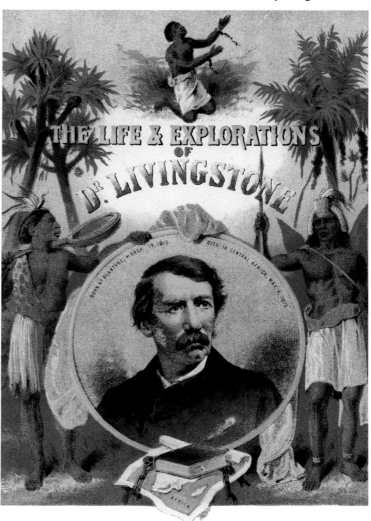

One of David Livingstone's greatest achievements as an explorer was following the course of the Zambezi River. He was the first European to see the river's enormous waterfall, which he called Victoria Falls after the British queen. The image of the freed slave at the top of this title page illustrates Livingstone's initial reason for exploring Africa—to end the slave trade.

"Doctor Livingstone, I Presume?"

African explorers were popular heroes in nineteenth-century Europe. No one enjoyed popularity more—or did more to place himself in the public eye—than Henry Morton Stanley. An ambitious reporter, Stanley persuaded an American newspaper to fund an expedition into Africa in search of the missionary-explorer David Livingstone. Because no word had come from Livingstone for more than a year, people began saying that he was lost. Stanley found him on the shore of Lake Tanganyika in 1871. According to Stanley's own book about the expedition, he greeted the missionary with the rather formal phrase, "Doctor Livingstone, I presume?" In reality Livingstone was not lost or in need of rescuing, but Stanley managed to present himself to the world as Livingstone's savior. Later Stanley made several ambitious and extremely dangerous journeys across Africa's last large unexplored region, the Congo River basin. His books about these adventures were best-sellers. Stanley mapped the course of the Congo River and urged the British government to establish a colony along it. When Britain showed no interest, Stanley helped King Leopold II of Belgium establish the Belgian Congo colony. Stanley later regretted his part in the founding of the Belgian Congo, which became the most exploitive and harshly governed European colony in Africa.

After writing a best-selling account of his meeting with Livingstone in the African jungle, reporter-turned-explorer Henry Morton Stanley focused his attention on the Congo River and rain forest. He crossed central Africa several times.

Explorers slowly solved the riddles of the rivers. In 1795–1796 Scotsman Mungo Park traveled along the Niger River and found that it was not a branch of the Nile. In 1858 British army officer John Hanning Speke discovered Lake Victoria in east Africa and claimed that it was the main source of the Nile—a claim that he proved on a second expedition by following the river all the way from the lake to the Mediterranean. Ptolemy's Mountains of the Moon were identified as the Ruwenzori Mountains of Uganda. By the end of the nineteenth century, Africa had been thoroughly mapped.

FORBIDDEN ASIA

Ringed on the north by deserts and on the south by the Himalayas, the world's highest mountain range, Tibet was one of the last parts of Asia to be explored by outsiders. Although early European travelers such as William of Rubruck and Marco Polo had written about Tibet, Europeans did not reach Lhasa, its capital, until some monks arrived there in 1661.

Beginning in the late eighteenth century, Europe took a new interest in Tibet and other little-known regions of central Asia. Russia had expanded its empire far into central Asia and Siberia, while Great Britain had claimed India as a colony. Between these two great powers lay Tibet and several other Himalayan kingdoms. Both Russia and Britain sent agents to map and spy on these lands "on the roof of the world." Tibet, however, had fallen under Chinese control, and China was determined to keep foreigners from entering the mountainous realm. Most intruders were turned back at the borders, but some were killed.

Britain solved the problem by training people from northern India in mapmaking and spying techniques. Disguised as religious pilgrims bound for Buddhist shrines, these native agents—called pundits from an Indian word for "learned ones"—made many highly dangerous journeys across the Himalayas and into the forbidden region. The Russians also entered Tibet from the north. The most successful Russian explorer was Nikolai Przhevalsky, who managed to map much of central Asia and northern Tibet but never made it to Lhasa. In 1899 a Russian student named Gombozhab Tsybikov, also disguised as a pilgrim, reached Lhasa and spent more than a year there. Alarmed by Russia's growing influence in Tibet, Britain sent a military expedition under Colonel Francis Younghusband to the region in 1904. After a fierce battle Younghusband

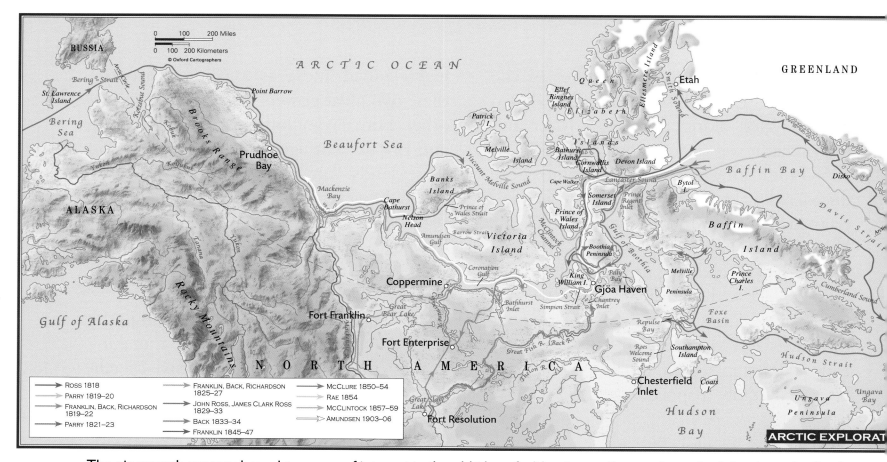

The nineteenth century brought a surge of interest in the old idea of a Northwest Passage from the Atlantic to the Pacific Ocean. Beginning with James Ross in 1818 and William Parry in 1819, a series of British explorers searched for the passage in the Canadian Arctic, part of Britain's Canadian colony. Sir John Franklin made three attempts to find the passage. He and all of his men died on the third journey, but the search for his remains led Robert McClure, John Rae, and Francis McClintock to map the water route through the Canadian Arctic. Norwegian explorer Roald Amundsen sailed that route in the early twentieth century.

reached Lhasa and forced the Tibetans into an alliance with Britain. Twenty years later a Frenchwoman named Alexandra David-Neel, using the tried-and-true pilgrim disguise, became the first Western woman to enter Lhasa. She returned to France and wrote best-selling books about Buddhism and her adventures in Asia.

THE FROZEN NORTH

Europeans began exploring the Arctic in the sixteenth century. They weren't particularly interested in its icebergs and polar bears. But they did desperately want to find the Northwest Passage—a fabled sea route that they thought would lead from the Atlantic through the northern part of the Americas all the way into the Pacific. Martin Frobisher searched the coast of Baffin Island for the passage in 1576–1578, and many others followed. The last of the early searches for the passage came in 1631–1632, when Thomas James looked in vain for a route west from Hudson Bay.

In 1845 Great Britain revived the search for the Northwest Passage by sending John Franklin, with 2 ships and 128 men, to sail through the uncharted waters of the Canadian Arctic. When the Franklin expedition failed to reappear, searchers fanned out through northern Canada and the Arctic islands. Eventually they learned that Franklin and all of his men had died after their ships had become stuck in the ice. Indirectly the search for Franklin resulted in a thorough exploration of the Arctic, during which a narrow, twisting, ice-choked route across the region was discovered. Although it was not the broad and easy passage Europeans had long dreamed of finding, Norwegian explorer Roald Amundsen managed to sail through it in 1903–1906.

But the biggest Arctic challenge proved to be the North Pole. In 1827 William Parry tried to reach it by crossing the polar ice cap. He failed, as did dozens of British, Italian, Norwegian, and American expeditions. Finally, in 1909, American Robert Peary claimed to have reached the pole. Seventeen years later Amundsen flew across the North Pole in a dirigible, and American Robert Byrd flew an airplane over it for the first time.

ANTARCTICA

The South Pole, locked in ice at the heart of a frozen and distant continent, was the last great trophy of world exploration. After James Cook discovered ice around the entire southern polar region, mariners of many nations tried to penetrate it. Not all of them were explorers. Some were American and British whalers and seal hunters, drawn to the wealth to be made in whale oil and sealskins harvested from the southernmost region of the earth. In 1820 expeditions from Russia, Britain, and the United States sighted portions of the Antarctic coast, and geographers became convinced that a continent lay trapped within that ice. Other expeditions mapped more of the coastline in the 1830s and 1840s, but serious Antarctic exploration began in 1895, when an interna-

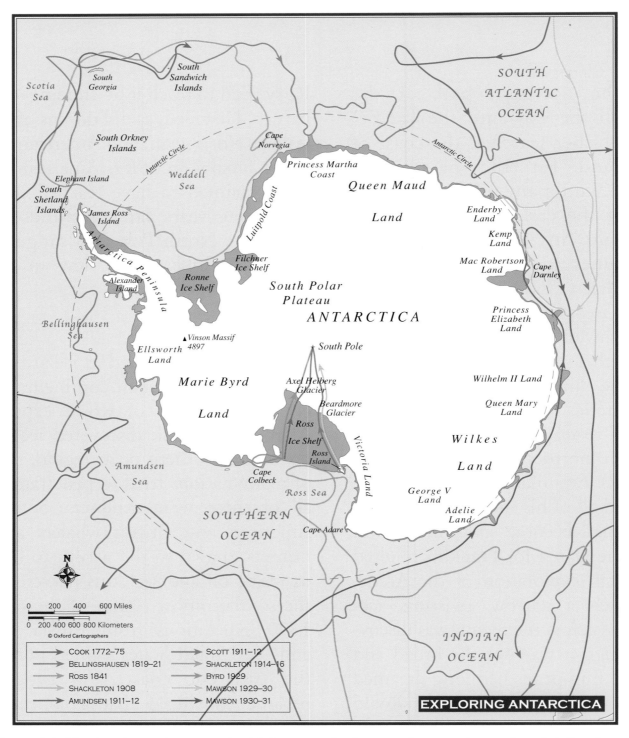

EXPLORING ANTARCTICA

SOUTH ATLANTIC OCEAN

Scotia Sea

South Georgia

South Sandwich Islands

South Orkney Islands

Antarctic Circle

Weddell Sea

Cape Norvegia

Princess Martha Coast

Queen Maud Land

Enderby Land

Kemp Land

Mac Robertson Land

Cape Darnley

Elephant Island

South Shetland Islands

James Ross Island

Antarctic Peninsula

Lutipold Coast

Filchner Ice Shelf

Alexander Island

Ronne Ice Shelf

South Polar Plateau

ANTARCTICA

Princess Elizabeth Land

Bellinghausen Sea

▲Vinson Massif 4897

Ellsworth Land

+ South Pole

Wilhelm II Land

Marie Byrd Land

Axel Heiberg Glacier

Beardmore Glacier

Ross Ice Shelf

Ross Island

Victoria Land

Queen Mary Land

Wilkes Land

Amundsen Sea

Cape Colbeck

George V Land

Ross Sea

Adelie Land

SOUTHERN OCEAN

Cape Adare

INDIAN OCEAN

N

0   200   400   600 Miles
0   200 400 600 800 Kilometers
© Oxford Cartographers

→ COOK 1772–75
→ BELLINGSHAUSEN 1819–21
→ ROSS 1841
→ SHACKLETON 1908
→ AMUNDSEN 1911–12
→ SCOTT 1911–12
→ SHACKLETON 1914–16
→ BYRD 1929
→ MAWSON 1929–30
→ MAWSON 1930–31

Antarctica, uninhabited and mostly covered with ice, was the last continent to be explored. A Russian admiral named Fabian Gottlieb von Bellingshausen sailed almost entirely around Antarctica between 1819 and 1821, mapping part of the coast. James Ross, a British naval captain who had already led Arctic expeditions, sailed to the coast of Victoria Land. The Ross Sea and Ross Ice Shelf were later named in his honor. Ernest Shackleton, Robert Falcon Scott, and Roald Amundsen competed to be the first person to reach the South Pole. American aviator Robert Byrd flew to the pole in 1929. Around the same time, Australian geologist Douglas Mawson made a wide-ranging geological survey of the continent and completed mapping its coastline.

Roald Amundsen of Norway was one of the most successful polar explorers. He was the first person to sail through the Northwest Passage as well as the first to reach the South Pole.

tional geographical conference called for an intensive study of the continent. During the next twenty-two years, nine countries sent sixteen major expeditions to Antarctica. A Belgian ship was the first to spend the winter there, while British, German, Scottish, French, and Swedish expeditions mapped the Antarctic Peninsula, the Ross Ice Shelf, and the Weddell Sea.

As with the North Pole, explorers felt intense pressure to be the first to reach the South Pole. Ernest Shackleton made the first dedicated attempt at the pole in a 1907–1909 expedition. He had to turn back 97 miles (156 kilometers) short of his goal. In 1911 Roald Amundsen and Englishman Robert Falcon Scott raced each other to the pole from opposite sides of the Ross Ice Shelf. Amundsen won the race, while Scott and his team perished on the return trip. A few years later Shackleton tried to become the first to cross the Antarctic continent. After ice crushed his ship, however, he had to abandon his plans. Instead of crossing Antarctica, Shackleton sailed a lifeboat across stormy Antarctic waters to the South Shetland Islands to get help for his men, whom he rescued from a camp on the Antarctic Peninsula. The heroic age of Antarctic exploration, as some historians call those years, produced epic achievements and stories of survival equal to those of Marco Polo and Ferdinand Magellan.

Glossary

archaeologist—One who studies ancient civilizations and cultures, usually by uncovering ruins.

caravan—A group of people traveling together for safety or convenience, usually with pack animals carrying goods.

circumnavigation—A journey around the world.

colony—A territory outside a state's borders that is controlled or claimed by that state.

empire—A large political organization that contains more than one ethnic or language group; usually created by force.

maritime—Related to the sea or sea travel.

navigation—The science of determining one's position on the earth's surface and following a course to a desired destination.

pilgrimage—A journey undertaken for a serious purpose, usually religious.

strait—A water passage between two landmasses.

c. 150 Greek scholar Ptolemy develops a system of mapmaking.

c. 1000 Vikings from Greenland visit the eastern coast of North America.

1295 Marco Polo returns to Italy from his travels in China and other parts of Asia.

1325–1349 Ibn Battūta travels through much of North Africa, the Near East, and Asia.

1405–1433 Chinese admiral Zheng He leads seven voyages to lands around the Indian Ocean.

1487 Bartolmeu Dias of Portugal sails around the tip of southern Africa.

1492–1504 Christopher Columbus, sailing for Spain, makes four voyages to the Americas.

1497 Vasco da Gama reaches India by sailing around Africa.

1522 One of Ferdinand Magellan's ships returns to Europe, completing the first voyage around the world.

1542 Francisco Orellana leads the first European expedition along the Amazon River in South America.

1728–1742 Vitus Bering leads Russian expeditions into the North Pacific and through northern Russia and Siberia.

1768–1779 James Cook makes three voyages into the Pacific, crossing the Arctic and Antarctic circles and discovering Hawaii.

1796 Scottish explorer Mungo Park reaches the Niger River in North Africa.

1804–1806 Meriwether Lewis and William Clark lead an American expedition from the Mississippi River to the Pacific Ocean and back.

1845–1848 A British Arctic expedition led by John Franklin disappears, leading to a flurry of exploration in the Canadian Arctic.

mid-1800s Native explorers called pundits survey and map Himalayan regions for the British.

1862 John Hanning Speke establishes Lake Victoria as the main source of the Nile River.

1874–1877 Henry Morton Stanley crosses Africa from east to west, charting the Congo River.

1903–1906 Roald Amundsen sails through the Northwest Passage.

1909 Robert Peary claims to reach the North Pole.

1911 Amundsen reaches the South Pole.

Chronology

Further Reading

BOOKS

Bohlander, Richard, ed. *World Explorers and Discoverers.* New York: Macmillan, 1992.

Ciovacco, Justine. *Encyclopedia of Explorers and Adventurers.* New York: Franklin Watts, 2003.

Fernández-Armesto, Felipe, ed. *Times Atlas of World Exploration.* New York: HarperCollins, 1992.

Gough, Barry, ed. *Geography and Exploration.* New York: Scribner, 2002. Volume 4 of Scribner's Science Reference Guide for young readers.

The Grolier Student Library of Explorers and Exploration. Danbury, CT: Grolier Educational, 1998. 10 volumes.

Konstam, Angus. *Historical Atlas of Exploration.* New York: Checkmark Books, 2000.

Matthews, Rupert. *The Explorer.* New York: Dorling Kindersley, 2000.

Saari, Peggy. *Explorers and Discoverers: From Alexander the Great to Sally Ride.* New York: UXL, 1995–1997. 6 volumes.

WEB SITES

www.memory.loc.gov/ammem/gmdhtml/dsxphome.html
The Library of Congress's Exploration and Discovery Home Page is a guide to maps and other exploration-related materials in the library's collections. It features many world maps made during the era of European world exploration as well as maps made during the 1700s and 1800s by explorers of North America.

www.mariner.org/age
The Mariners' Museum in Newport News, Virginia, maintains the Age of Exploration site, a study and teaching guide about seagoing exploration from ancient times to James Cook's first Pacific voyage in 1768.

www.library.thinkquest.org/C001692
The Voyage of Exploration: Discovering New Horizons site includes biographies of many explorers, a time line, information on navigation through the ages, and other resources.

www.ucalgary.ca/applied_history/tutor/eurvoya/
Canada's University of Calgary maintains the European Voyages of Exploration, a site that introduces students to the motives, events, and consequences of Portuguese and Spanish voyages in the 1400s and 1500s.

www.jacksoneds.k12.or.us/k12projects/jimperry/explorers.html
History Online: Exploration and Discovery is a collection of links to many sites dealing with explorers and exploration.

www.win.tue.nl/cs/fm/engels/discovery/index.html
The home page of the Discoverers Web offers an enormous number of links to sites about explorers and exploration; links are arranged by historical period and also by world region.

ABOUT THE AUTHOR

Rebecca Stefoff is the author of Marshall Cavendish's North American Historical Atlases series, the *Young Oxford Companion to Maps and Mapmaking,* and many other nonfiction books for children and young adults, including the three-volume Extraordinary Explorers series: *Accidental Explorers, Women of the World,* and *Scientific Explorers* (Oxford University Press, 1992). Stefoff wrote the Explorers volume for *Grolier's Library of North American Biographies* (1994) and is also the author of *Ferdinand Magellan and the Discovery of the World Ocean* (Chelsea House, 1990), *Marco Polo and the Medieval Explorers* (Chelsea House, 1992), *Vasco da Gama and the Portuguese Explorers* (Chelsea House, 1993), and *The Viking Explorers* (Chelsea House, 1993). She makes her home in Portland, Oregon. Visit her Web site at www.rebeccastefoff.com.

Index

Page numbers in **boldface** are illustrations.